FOREVER MY COMPANION
(MEA ANGELUS)

Published by

Sophia Books, Malaparamba,
Kozhikode, Kerala, India- 673 009.
+91 495 2373077, +91 9995574308
www.sophiabuy.com

A Christian Book Publisher dedicated to furthering
the work of Christ through the written word.

ISBN: 978-93-84884-17-8
Price: ₹ 299/-, Out of India: $8.99, £6
SB 183 | IE 2000 | April 2016

Printed in India by
National Printing Press, Bengaluru.

FOREVER MY COMPANION

"I am with you always,
until the end of the age" (Mt. 28:20)

NEENA ABRAHAM

Illustration
ARUN ANTONY & ABHILASH G DEVAN

It was night. Teresa sat on her bed. She took her favorite book to read. She couldn't focus. She looked out through the window. The sky was cloudy and the moon was barely visible. She felt sad and lonely. She missed her old home. Her family had just moved to a town named Joyville.

Today was her first day at the new school. She remembered her old friends. Having lunch together... playing together... She ate her lunch alone. As usual her mom left a note in her lunch bag. She read it to herself. "I am with you always, until the end of the age."

"Teresa", she heard her mom calling. "It's time to sleep."

Mom walked into her room.
"Are you ok, sweetheart?" mom asked.
"I am fine." Teresa said.
"Don't worry. I know you miss our old
home and friends." Teresa couldn't hide her
tears. "Teresa..." mom looked at
her eyes and wiped her tears.
She put her hands over her shoulder and
said in a tender voice. "Teresa... Offer
everything to your loving Father and take
this from His hands. Listen to His voice."
"I am with you always, until the end of
the age." Teresa smiled at her mom and
said, "Let me get ready for bed."

Teresa brushed her teeth, took a bath and slipped into her pajamas.

She saw her treasure bag on top of the chest. Her thoughts went back to her old town and friends. Tears filled her eyes and rolled down.

Suddenly she heard the inner voice. "I am with you always, until the end of the age." Mom always told her that nothing happens in our life without God's permission.

"Teresa... You must sleep now" She heard her mom calling.

Teresa came back to her room. She knelt down with her mom for prayer. "Thank you Jesus, for everything, the joy, the sorrow, and all the blessings. I am sorry for hurting You. Thank you for being with me when I felt lonely..."

Teresa saw the picture of the Holy Family.

"Mother Mary and St. Joseph must have felt lonely when they left the town of Nazareth and went to Bethlehem to give birth to Jesus." Teresa rambled in her thoughts again... But it strengthened her.

"Mom, I can also offer my little troubles to Jesus." Teresa said to her mom.

"You are indeed so dear to Jesus." Mom gave her a hug.

"I am with you always, until the end of the age." Teresa remembered about the lunch note. "Thank you mom." Teresa kissed her mom Goodnight and laid on her bed.

Shining stars... They were looking at her and smiling. They were dancing and singing glory to God. She wished she had wings to fly and join the stars. Suddenly, she noticed a bright star coming closer and closer to her.

She awoke with a start, "I'm flying with the stars." she thought.

No, she was still in her bed. But the star was coming towards her window."

Wait! It wasn't a star. It came through the window and stood by her bedside. She smelled a beautiful fragrance. It was very bright and had two wings. It came closer to Teresa and placed its hands over her. The touch was so delicate.

Teresa asked, "Who are you?"

"I am your Angelus."

"Angelus?" Teresa wondered.

"Your Guardian Angel, Teresa," Angelus said,

"You know my name?" Teresa was surprised.

"Of course, I am with you all the time protecting and guiding you" Angelus replied.

"My Guardian Angel!" Teresa wondered.

"Yes, your friend and guardian" Angelus told Teresa.

“Where were you all these days?” Teresa asked.

I was walking next to you, and sometimes carrying you in my arms.” Angelus said.

“Really! Who sent you now?” Teresa asked.

“Your loving God.” Angelus replied.

“My Loving God?” Teresa heard the voice again in her heart.

“I am with you always, until the end of the age”.

"He was always walking beside you." Angelus said.

"My Lord was walking with me for real?" Teresa couldn't hide her excitement.

"Yes, Teresa. You are so special to Him." Angelus said.

"He loves you so much and you are close to His heart." Angelus said.

Teresa thought about the words. "I am with you always, until the end of the age".

"I love Him so much too." Teresa said. "I love Him above everything."

"I miss my old friends." Teresa said.

"You will have many friends soon." Angelus said.

"But..." Teresa wanted to say something. Before she could finish, Angelus told her, "Don't worry. You have many friends in heaven. Your Father in heaven loves you so much. You are His special child."

"I am with you always, until the end of the age." She heard the inner voice.

Angelus told, "Teresa, you came here for a purpose. It was not an accident."

"My mom tells me this all the time, but I don't understand." Teresa replied.

"There will be multiple paths in front of you. But if you choose the one from God, you will be dear to Him." Angelus said.

"How do I know which one is from God?" Teresa asked.

"Don't worry. He will always reveal it to you." Angelus said.

"I am with you always, until the end of the age." Teresa heard the inner voice again.

"Am I here because of His plan?" Teresa asked.

"Of course. You are His chosen one." Angelus replied.

"What? The chosen one?" Teresa wondered.

"He has a special call for you." Angelus continued. "Everyone has a special call. But only a few respond to that call." Angelus said.

"I want to respond to His call. But sometimes I feel so weak and sad." Teresa said.

"Listen to His voice in your heart." Angelus said.

"I am with you always, until the end of the age." Teresa heard.

"I will do whatever He asks me to do." Teresa said.

"That is indeed very true. That's why He loves you so much. He will ask you to do bigger things for Him." Angelus said.

"Bigger things! But..." Teresa wanted to say something.

"Trust in Him completely. Give your weakness to Him. He will strengthen you." Angelus told her.

"I am with you always, until the end of the age." Teresa listened to her inner voice.

"You will be a soldier of Christ." Angelus told her.

"Soldier... me? Teresa couldn't hide her excitement.

"Like Saint Joan of Arc?" Teresa asked.

"You will fight like Joan of Arc. But an invisible fight." Angelus said.

"Invisible fight! I will be scared." Teresa wondered.

"No Teresa, He will protect you."

Teresa heard "I am with you always, until the end of the age."

"You will be fighting against this world. You will be a part of the army of God's Kingdom. I will train you to become a good fighter." Angelus said.

"In your struggles, in your sadness, in your happiness always remember your loving Father." Angelus continued.

"I am with you always, until the end of the age."

Teresa didn't like fighting.

"I am not a fighter at all." Teresa said.

"Don't worry. You are already a little fighter of Jesus." Angelus said.

"How? I don't understand." Teresa said.

"You responded to His call by obeying your parents. You happily accepted the troubles and sadness." Angelus said.

"Really! I am a warrior of God, He trains me?"

Teresa heard the voice, "I am with you always, until the end of the age."

Angelus took Teresa back to her bed and sat beside her. "There will be many battles for you to fight." Angelus placed his hands over Teresa's forehead and continued. "Now go to sleep and we will talk about it later." Angelus got up from the bed.

"Angelus, can you please stay with me?" Teresa asked. Angelus held her hand and promised. "Sure. I am going to be with you. I will come whenever you call me."

Teresa closed her eyes and fell asleep.

"I am with you always, until the end of the age." She kept repeating in her sleep.

Teresa woke up from her sleep and sat on the bed. She looked out through the window. The sun was rising… The sky was clear. She heard the birds singing…

Teresa thanked God for the new day. She asked for the protection of her Guardian Angel.

"Guardian Angel… Angelus… A dream!" Teresa wondered. "I am with you always, even until the end of this Age". Teresa again heard the whisper.

Teresa was ready to begin her battle as a little soldier. Her heart filled with hope and faith in Christ.

"Mom…" Teresa called her mom, "I saw angelus." She ran to the kitchen…